The modern method of selling

How to sell like a pro

By

Jason T. Patton

Table of contents

Introduction

Everyone has something they can sell, whether it's a service, a product, or useful information.

However, gaining customers and increasing sales from that service, product, or information is the only way a business can succeed.

You can't just hope that people will find your product and buy it.

An increase in sales is the result of well-thought-out sales strategies that are planned and carried out, not something that just happens. You need to either increase the number of customers you are selling to, enhance what you are selling, improve your messaging, or do all of the above in order to increase sales, particularly your sales at the end of the year.

You will be able to comprehend how you can assist your ideal customer once you are certain that you have a comprehensive understanding of their issues, needs, and desires.

What issue is addressed by your product or service? How does it address your customer's issue?

They will buy from you if you have correctly identified your customer and know how your product solves their problem. But the customer you've identified won't buy your product if they don't have this issue.

Serving people with what they want and them been willing to pay more than someone else is the key to all great success and fortune. You can learn how to serve people and provide exceptional customer service by adopting a mindset of "help" rather than "sell."

Giving potential customers something truly exceptional—for free—is one strategy for demonstrating your company's value to them. Offering freebies to warm leads who aren't quite ready to buy your actual product is a great way to build trust. They will be much more likely to purchase once they see what you have to offer in action.

Your actual product or service can serve as a sample for this freebie, or it can be something that complements it. Make sure that your freebie is valuable on its own, regardless of what it is; This is how you build trust with your leads, get them excited about the next step, and actually make a sale. You should read this book if making sales has been difficult for you despite numerous attempts.

This book is for you if you're avoiding sales conversations because you're afraid of being rejected or don't know what to do.

Chapter 1

Knowing how to sell.

Any transaction in which money is exchanged for a good or service is considered selling. The buyer will give the seller money in exchange for the seller's product or service if they want to make a deal. Simply put, selling is the process of persuading others.

Even though there are good and bad salespeople, the act of selling does not depend on how well the seller does. Instead, regardless of whether a deal is reached, "selling" simply refers to the attempt to sell a product or service for money. For instance, when you enter a department store, you will see dozens of product aisles. While the store is attempting to sell you everything in its inventory, you may only select one item. In that store, every display, discount, and salesperson is trying to sell you something. All sales deals are not the same. Purchasing a vehicle is very different from purchasing gas for your vehicle.

There is no need for persuasion when buying gas when the tank is empty for the first time. On the other hand, most of the time, there is no immediate need to buy a car. It usually requires the assistance of a salesperson and requires a larger investment to obtain.

How Selling Works

When you're trying to sell a product or service, you need to emphasize the benefits to the customer. Solutions and products are bought by people who believe they will improve their lives, make them happier, or satisfy a particular need.

For instance, if you're selling insurance for long-term care, the customer should be aware of the high costs of long-term care and the advantages of not having to worry about paying for it. The buyer needs to know how the product or service will make their lives better or fulfill a need.

Requirements for selling

Selling is essential to a company's success, but many people find it daunting. Fortunately, it is possible to learn how to sell without being arrogant or obnoxious. To be a successful salesperson, you need the following qualities and abilities:

* The capacity to form individual, long-term relationships with customers:

The majority of successful salespeople consider long-term strategies for converting the current sale into the additional business from the same client or through referrals.

*The capacity to pay attention to the client:

Too many salespeople attempt to persuade potential customers to buy without first determining what the customer actually wants. Solutions or items that make them feel good are purchased by customers. If you don't know what the customer wants or needs, you can't do that.

*Tenacity: A good salesperson never gives up on a potential customer and is aware that it may take several attempts to close the deal. Instead, they have a system for following up with potential customers. A reminder via email or phone call might close the deal in the future.

*Self-motivation: People who are successful in sales take a lot of initiative. They always look for new opportunities and see challenges as opportunities to learn. They hold themselves accountable for their performance and do not attribute failure to others or the current economic climate.

*Self-promotion: This might entail giving out business cards and other promotional materials, making a website, posting on social media, and developing and using an email list.

*Putting money into the community: It is not only good for the soul but also for businesses to give back to the community in which they work by sponsoring community groups, donating to charities, and volunteering. When you give back to the community, your customers are more likely to do so when they need your products or services.

Types of Selling

There are a variety of strategies and systems for selling, some of which work and some of which should be avoided. Some of the necessary ways are:

1. Sales under pressure: People often tell salespeople that buyers are liars and that they need to push hard and not take "no" for an answer to get the sale. However, the majority of buyers do not want to be coerced. High-pressure sales typically fail or result in regrettable purchases.

2. Selling on a transaction: This strategy focuses on selling quickly; There is no effort made to establish a long-term relationship with the client. Although transactional selling is frequently derided, it does have its place. From the perspective of the customer, sometimes all they want or need is a straightforward transaction. For instance, purchasing a new outfit or car gas: This strategy focuses on selling quickly; There is no effort made to establish a long-term relationship with the client. Although transactional selling is frequently derided, it does have its place. From the perspective of the customer, sometimes all they want or need is a straightforward transaction. For instance, purchasing a new outfit or car gas.

3. Relationship selling (consultative selling): The customer's ongoing relationship is at the heart of this strategy. The goal of the salesperson is to learn about the customer's wants and needs so they can give the customer what they want best.

4. Selling together:

By fostering a partnership between the seller and the buyer, this method of selling goes one step further than relationship selling. The buyer must have a lot of faith that the seller will always put their needs first.

The approach you should take is determined by your personality, business, and clientele. You will probably be more successful in sales as a result of your greater comfort with certain selling styles as a salesperson.

Because their products are automatically sold, founders and marketers should first concentrate on the need (the benefit) and how it will affect the customer.

The story, the concept, its benefits, comfort, authenticity, and a status symbol are what make a product expensive, not the raw materials you put into it.

skills in sales that help some of the best salespeople in the world succeed.

1. Having an understanding of what your customer wants.

Having an understanding of what the buyer needs Understanding the buyer is the foundation of effective selling, but understanding the buyer requires more than just knowing who the buyer is. Instead, it's about figuring out what the buyer wants to do when they think about buying something in your market.

Your job as a salesperson is to meet or exceed the expectations of your customer regarding that experience. If you don't know what the buyer wants from their experience, you can't go above and beyond them.

2. Sell in a way that is responsive to the buyer

when a salesperson knows who the customer is, they can use buyer-responsive selling. This is all about giving the customer what they want when they want it. Give your buyer a free trial that is simple to set up, easy to use, and demonstrates the value of your product in five minutes or less if, for instance, they require a trial to evaluate your product but cannot devote more than 30 minutes to it.

3. Engage the buyer through psychology

There are a variety of psychological strategies you can employ to cultivate a deeper level of engagement with your target audience. It's a good idea to let the customer know that you won't waste their time too much.

4. Build trust with the buyer

Buyers prefer to do business with trustworthy individuals. The ability to build trust with customers is a crucial selling skill for good salespeople.

5. Simplify your communication

Buyers often place more importance on how information is presented than the information itself. Never try to cover more than three important points in a single conversation with a buyer.

6. Demonstrate expertise in the subject matter

Salespeople must comprehend the buyer, including the pressing issues they face and their desires as they work toward a purchase. Additionally, they must be knowledgeable about both their own product or service and the market.

7. Tell compelling stories about your product or service

This is something that good salespeople are aware of, and they incorporate the product or service they are selling into a larger narrative with an arc that leads to the customer receiving what they want, which is typically not your product. For instance, a company doesn't really want to buy a phone system; rather, they want to increase revenue and are aware that a phone is a useful tool for doing so.

8. Develop your skills as a copywriter

Salespeople need to be able to write. Given how frequently buyers communicate with sales via email, this is one of the most important sales skills in today's market. When writing sales copy, there are a few things to keep in mind:

*It's better to write less. Make an effort to keep written communications succinct.

*Do not employ generic copy. Make an effort to personalize as many of your communications as you can.

*For formatting your copy, use bullets. Customers simply find lists easier to understand.

*Last but not least, begin and end each of your written communications with a call to action that prompts the customer to take a subsequent action.

9. Sell effectively over the phone

Field sales are moving inside, and the 60-minute teleconference is quickly replacing face-to-face meetings. Salespeople must therefore be able to effectively manage sales calls over the phone.

This necessitates a variety of skills, such as the capacity to gauge a person's level of satisfaction by analyzing their voice tone or the conversation's cadence.

10. Engage socially with potential customers

Social media has spawned the field of social selling. Participation on social media platforms like Facebook, Twitter, and LinkedIn is seen as one of the most important sales skills by many salespeople. Some of the best salespeople host dinner parties for groups of customers they want to get to know. These mini-events have very little sales activity.

11. Create intimate interactions

Buyers don't want a generic sales pitch or message; They are looking for something that is unique to them. Integrating messaging and content tailored to the demographics of your customers into your sales efforts is one way to achieve this.

On the side of the customer, you might have to adjust how you talk to them based on their age and gender. Depending on the context of the sale, you can also personalize your interactions by making reference to recent happenings in the buyer's personal or professional lives.

12. Make use of a variety of marketing abilities

Salespeople who possess advanced marketing abilities typically do well. Content selling, for instance, is a crucial skill that salespeople can use to guide customers through the buying process.

Many sales activities are being structured in a way that looks like a campaign, which sales management is taking from marketing. For instance, some businesses are structuring the manner in which they carry out conventional sales activities like prospecting by employing a campaign format.

13. Assist prospects in completing their next steps

It is no longer sufficient to agree on the next steps; you must actually assist the buyer in completing those next steps. Let's say a buyer with whom you've been collaborating needs to get the CEO's okay before they can make a decision. You should give the buyer the content, tools, and information they need to convince the CEO that your product or service is right.

14. Make use of technology in sales to increase productivity

A lot of sales organizations use technology to become more effective and reduce the average length of a sales cycle. Salespeople who are able to increase their productivity through technology have a significant advantage over their colleagues because they can spend more time selling.

15. Treat their pipeline as if it were a portfolio.

The most effective salespeople manage their pipeline like a portfolio manager would. They devote time to a number of opportunities, knowing that not all will succeed. On a daily or weekly basis, they monitor the performance of each opportunity and their entire pipeline as a whole. Additionally, they can at any time carry out a "bottoms up" analysis of their pipeline to ascertain where they stand in relation to their quota target.

Chapter 2

Sales Myths and the Reality of Sales

Every week, salespeople encounter a plethora of obstacles and objections. The public's perception of the so-called "salesperson" is one of the biggest barriers that salespeople face on a weekly basis.

If they believe the person on the other end of the phone is just trying to sell them something, a lot of people are more likely to hang up.

However, this does not imply that selling or employing selling strategies is a bad thing. In fact, that is one of the most prevalent sales myths: that you must act in a different capacity than a seller in order to gain access.

The modern method of selling

Ten Myths About Selling to Customers (Along with the Real Truth)

1. The Myth That the Customer Is Always Right

This is one of the most common misconceptions among sales and customer service professionals. It was initially intended to motivate employees to concentrate on satisfying customers and prioritizing their requirements. This myth can cause salespeople to believe that they must agree with every request a customer makes, or it can cause customers to be told what they want to hear even when a brand's solution is not right for them. The reality is that not everyone is a good fit for your business, so you need to be willing to reach out to people but also move on to customers who are better suited when a market doesn't work for you.

2. Selling is filthy and dishonest.

I believe that the most widespread misconception is that selling is somehow dirty and unworthy. Since money is never taught to medical residents, they believe that selling used cars is only for them when they graduate. However, it is a blessing to sell products that benefit others. You are blessing people by selling, and that's nothing to be ashamed of.

3. They will arrive if you build them.

is a well-known adage that is used to propagate a widespread myth. Before making a purchase, today's customers are looking for the value that your product or service provides.

. Therefore, you ought to consider the following: "If you provide value, they will buy." First, consider the most frequently asked questions about your product or service. After that, create content to answer those questions and distribute it to your customers. The foundation is establishing trust and a relationship. After that, sales will take place. People want to buy from services that have helped them and from people they know and like. Humans feel obligated to assist you back if you assist them. As a result, they will purchase your item or service and recommend you to others. After you have provided sufficient value, you can request the sale of their business. Focus on being the most valuable.

4. Fully automated sales are possible.

The widespread misconception that the majority of the selling process can be scientifically defined and automated is one of the most common today. Customers prefer a human connection, even though a lot of scheduling and communication can be accelerated with tools. The human connection enables us to believe and invest in the purchase alongside another human, whether it's a smile from the barista who delivers your favorite mid-morning drink or a text message from a salesperson proposing to overhaul your customer experience process. The reality of sales is that they occur constantly; We are trading ideas, ways of being, and our trustworthiness for each other. - Just because we can communicate behind screens and concentrate on our devices does not mean we should.

5. A great product is self-promoting.

The widespread misconception is that if you have a great product or service, customers will buy it and keep buying it. Businesses still need to reach customers despite the fact that revolutionary ideas do occur. The majority of businesses operate in highly competitive environments where numerous products or services meet similar needs. Therefore, the real difference lies in how effectively the company implements and comprehends customer orientation. Most products and services' long-term success will be determined by the client's perception of genuine care and effort put into the relationship, not by the products or services themselves. This is evidently even more significant and pronounced in professional services. Regardless of how virtual things are becoming, customer orientation is the future of sales.

6. Always Close The Sale

Always Be Closing the Sale" is a dangerous sales myth. In the world of sales, this is a well-known saying. However, as your pipeline grows, your top employees may overpromise just to meet their sales quota. Sales managers are directly accountable for acquiring new customers, regardless of the consequences of losing existing ones. This will unavoidably result in an increase in support time on a large scale, possibly promising the world to customers who do not receive sufficient value, which will ultimately damage your brand reputation. Create excellent sales guidelines that prevent you from selling more than you can afford. For best results, instead, focus on underpromising and exceeding expectations.

7. The item must be the best

The myth that your product must be the best is that it must be one of the best. In fact, people are more likely to buy something that makes them feel how they want to feel than they are to buy the product that is made the best or has the lowest price. For instance, people frequently make purchases based on what others are purchasing. The newcomer will win the sale if a celebrity uses the product or if the product is thought to be "popular" among people the consumer admires. The most important lesson is to focus on how your product or service makes potential customers feel. Customers will buy from you if you can convey the mood they desire. However, you run the risk of missing out on a significant opportunity if you only concentrate on the product's functionality rather than its perception.

8. Salespeople are aggressive and talk quickly.

The most common misconception about selling to customers is those successful salespeople are high-energy, fast-talking, and aggressive. The old cliche that salespeople should "always be closing" in order to be successful is the source of this myth. In today's hyper-connected world of social media, the best salespeople don't talk the most during a sales conversation. Before offering a particular solution to a customer, the best salespeople conduct a thorough analysis of the customer's real issues, aspirations, and roadblocks by asking as many questions as possible. Contrarily, this "diagnose before you prescribe" strategy enables great salespeople to close more sales because it makes your customer feel heard and understood rather than "talked at."

9. Have a Plan for Selling

My biggest selling myth is that you need to use old "sales techniques" to get a sale. When I first started my business, I thought you needed a sales script to close sales calls. Selling became simple for me once I concentrated on creating social proof and emotional connections with my ideal client through my content and communication. Some people believe that you need sales training to sell, but all you need is an offer that solves the problems of your ideal customer, social proof that sells for you, and credibility that you have built up with them through all of your communication. Selling becomes simple if you begin your business with people you know, like, and trust. People purchase From those they know, like, and can put their trust on.

10. The Success of a Sale Depends on the First Three Minutes

Although first impressions are important, you won't know if you've closed the deal in those first three minutes. Everyone is unique, and many customers decide to buy once they feel at ease with the salesperson. Apply that attention to establishing a

The modern method of selling

relationship with the customer by engaging them in conversation and asking them pertinent questions to help you better position your pitch rather than focusing on any arbitrary time limit suggested by this sales myth.

11. There is no need for businesses to sell because marketing alone can generate orders

It could be argued that in our ever-expanding online world, certain commodities, inexpensive items, and other products are bought rather than sold. This may be true for some consumer goods or low-value business purchases, but in order for any business to expand into any market segment, someone will need to pitch and sell ideas to partners, retailers, and others.

Face-to-face sales continue even in these instances. Face-to-face selling is a skill that every business with high-value products or high order values must master in order to expand quickly.

Because the customer can now find a lot more information online before any sales are made, sales teams are smaller than they were a decade ago. As a result, the salesperson's role has evolved to become more consultative, advisory, and value-adding.

This change presents a fantastic opportunity for you as a scale-up entrepreneur because building your sales team is now more about quality than quantity. In the beginning, you should concentrate on building a high-quality, specialized sales team made up of you and one or two other talented, driven, and dependable salespeople who are regarded by customers as reliable advisers.

12. High-performing salespeople are always the result of skilled recruitment and training.

Hiring a successful salesperson does not guarantee success in sales. In a similar vein, enrolling a salesperson in a tried-and-true course does not guarantee their success. There are few guarantees in sales, which makes it interesting and difficult!

It could be similar to Real Madrid paying a lot of money to sign a star striker and making sure the player gets the right training, coaching, and development. They ought to perform well and score many goals, but that never happens!

Your company will need to hire and train employees but do so in a thoughtful, cost-effective manner that fits your entrepreneurial culture. People will perform better if they feel like they are an integral part of a close-knit team, so it's important to get the people to get along well.

Put sales at the center of your expansion. This reality check might have given you some real surprises. But the most important thing is that I hope it has given you a better understanding of what modern, professional selling is and isn't.

The debunking of these myths demonstrates that anyone can become an effective salesperson and that, as an entrepreneur, there are absolutely no obstacles in your way, to begin with, founder selling and then develop a potent sales engine for expanding your business.

You have a great chance to improve your sales skills and build a great sales team, both of which will help your business grow and give you the momentum you need to expand successfully.

Chapter 3

The most significant issue in sales.

Every sales representative wants to celebrate their victories at the end of the month. Sadly, however, the majority of sales representatives are left disappointed when their targets are not met. Problems that have an impact on sales results frequently confront sales representatives. The problem is that sales representatives ignore these obstacles and continue to sell, resulting in the same disappointing monthly sales results.

Look for a way through the obstacle, not a way out.

Common obstacles in sales and how to overcome them

No one, not even the best salespeople, is immune to obstacles. However, rather than ignoring the difficulties in sales, they address them. Take on the challenges so that you can experience victory's exhilaration.

The most typical difficulties that the majority of sales representatives face, along with solutions, are listed below.

Problem 1 in sales: Keeping up with rivals

The market has transformed into a battlefield where businesses are doing everything in their power to outperform their rivals. This is the first sales challenge. Competitors are experimenting with a variety of strategies to entice customers, including price reductions and freebies.

These are the points that potential buyers choose to use as a shield to get the product at a lower price. Statements such as "The [X competitor] is offering a product at a much lower price" or "The [Y competitor] is giving four months free subscription to their service" are heard by the majority of sales representatives.

When faced with such inquiries, the majority of sales representatives either lose their minds or make a rash decision that hurts their profits.

Solutions

*After conducting a thorough competitive analysis, map out the strengths and weaknesses of the competitors.

*Demonstrate to your potential customers how you stand out from your rivals.

* Provide case studies and testimonials from content clients who chose you over your rivals.

Problem 2 in sales: not enough time to sell

from gathering information about a potential customer to writing sales emails and updating records, a sales representative must complete a lot in a single day. In addition, if things aren't organized, searching for information consumes more time. Sales representatives lack sufficient time to concentrate on selling and strategizing.

Sales representatives actually sell for 35.2% of their time.

Solutions

*Use an automation tool to automate the majority of your tasks.

* Make use of tools with profile enrichment features to automatically retrieve vital information about your prospects.

*Instead of writing each email from scratch, create and use email templates.

* Utilize sales reports to keep track of your sales activities and prioritize your week's tasks.

*Instead of using diaries and notes, select a single platform to store all of your customer data.

The problem in sales 3: not receiving a response from the prospect.

After a few initial interactions, the majority of prospects stop responding.

This silence demotivates a number of sales representatives. They start concentrating on a different prospect instead of the lead. As a result, the majority of leads do not become customers.

Solution:

*Continually pursue your goals without giving up. To automate the follow-up, you can make use of tools that let you create email and text sequences.

*In order to get more responses, write content and subject lines for your emails that are engaging.

*Find a way to get in touch with someone from the prospect's company.

* Meet with the prospect at various times. Determine the optimal time to call or email the prospect.

*Connect with your prospects via text messages and social media sites in addition to calls and emails.

The problem in sales 4:Reluctance of the prospects during the negotiation

The majority of sales deals are lost during the negotiation phase of the process, which is sales challenge number four. A number of prospects are unwilling to reach an agreement or make concessions. In addition, the sales reps are irritated by the prospect's reluctance, and as a result, they end up expressing their anger in an unpleasant manner. Solution:

*Be calm throughout the negotiation and consider your options before responding to a customer's objection.

*Discover and experiment with various strategies for negotiating with reluctant prospects.

* Find the areas of stress for the prospects and make them imagine what would happen if they didn't address the issue right away.

*The initial quote was too high. Then provide a low price and few features. Make the actual proposal while the prospect is choosing between two offers.

Problem in sales 5: Unable to deal with criticism or rejection.

The majority of sales representatives are unable to accept criticism or hear a "NO." They lose motivation. This event has an effect on their next deal because they can't concentrate on communicating because they were disappointed by the rejection or criticism.

Solution:

*Rehearse and prepare a persuasive response for when you receive a no.

*Don't let your emotions control you; work on improving your EQ (emotional intelligence).

*To get you ready to deal with rejection on sales calls, ask your senior to conduct a practice call.

*Make a lot of chances for yourself so that you won't be hurt by many rejections.

The problem in sales 6: Sales Education

The majority of businesses have high expectations, but they don't give their salespeople the right training to deal with today's smart buyers. Low sales productivity is primarily caused by a lack of training. The majority of the agents have trouble reaching their sales targets.

Solution:

*Request funding for training from management by locating the areas where it is required.

*Watch live webinars to hear from experts in the field.

*Demand regular performance evaluations from senior citizens.

The problem in sales 7: Not enough time to prospect

A critical phase of the sales process is prospecting. However, prospecting takes up a lot of time for the majority of sales representatives. Regular cold calls can introduce you to numerous lucrative opportunities. Therefore, don't put off this crucial sales task.

Solution:

*Define a time frame for each day's cold calls.

*To cut down on time and work more efficiently, use a power dialer.

*For any other task, you should not ignore the cold calling.

The problem in sales 8: Not being able to answer questions from prospects.

Today's buyers are very smart and well-informed. They keep up with the most recent technologies and market trends. As a result, they frequently ask many questions. Sales representatives frequently lose their

minds and are unable to respond to these inquiries. Do you have this problem as well? If so, the following actions need to be taken:
Solution:

*First and foremost, make sure you know a lot about the product.
*Create a list of frequently asked questions and prepare for them.
*Conduct a mock call with your senior.
The majority of sales representatives face price as their greatest obstacle. Many other price-based obstacles include the price being too high, not being clear, being out of budget, and so on.
Redirecting the discussion from price to value is the best strategy for overcoming this obstacle. You could, for instance, ask, "How would it change things for you tomorrow if we implemented this for you today?" You can get potential customers to focus on the value your product or service will bring by focusing on a short or immediate timeline like this or another suitable timeline.
The majority of sales representatives should be able to offer pricing or payment terms with flexibility if value-focused selling is unsuccessful. This

adaptability could accompany various levels of contributions, or even the capacity to say, "OK, I can make this work for your spending plan assuming you sign by Friday." Your reps' close rates and success greatly improve when they are given such authority.

Chapter 4

Keeping customers' attention

Building an effective customer focus strategy and gaining a deeper understanding of customer focus are the first steps toward improving your customer focus.

Your customers are scrutinizing your business more closely than ever before because they have higher expectations than ever before. They are contrasting your brand's experience with the simple, quick, and personalized ones they have had with the best of the best. Additionally, businesses that place a strong emphasis on their clients stand to gain a competitive advantage and rekindle customer loyalty.

Customer focus has never been more important because 89% of businesses compete primarily on customer experience. However, there is still a gap between the percentage of customers who agree and the percentage of businesses that believe they are customer-focused. In point of fact, only 8% of customers agree with the assertion that 80% of businesses provide "super experiences."

The good news is that improving customer focus is possible. Additionally, it begins with developing an efficient customer-focus strategy and expanding your comprehension of the term "customer focus."

How does customer focus work?

Putting your customers' needs first is customer focus. Businesses that are focused on their customers cultivate a work environment that is focused on increasing customer contentment and fostering long-term relationships with them.

However, it is not solely the responsibility of customer support or any one team to achieve customer focus for the entire company. Customer-focused businesses demonstrate that the customer experience matters throughout the organization, at every stage of the customer journey, despite the fact that customer service skills are essential to customer focus.

Customer focus is the lens through which you analyze all of your interactions with your customers. "It's a core value for who you want to be as a company and how you want your customers to feel about you," the honesty of their marketing campaigns, the transparency of their pricing models, the ease of their sales cycle, and the quality of their actual products or services.

The significance of customer focus

Customer focus is the basis for customer loyalty because it demonstrates to your clients that you will prioritize their needs. 74% of customers say they are devoted to a single business, and 52% say they go above and beyond to buy from their preferred brands.

In addition, approximately half of the customers indicate that one negative experience would lead them to switch to a competitor. In addition, this percentage rises to 80% when there are multiple negative experiences. It is essential to transform your business into a customer-centric one if you want to ensure that customers leave with a positive impression of your brand. This is due to the fact that you will need to view them as the driving force behind everything you do.

putting the needs of the customer first is crucial to developing more genuine relationships with them. This entails gaining knowledge from your clients and applying those valuable insights to improve.

Tips for Creating an Effective Customer Focus Strategy

Building an Effective Customer Focus Strategy consists of two levels: the operational level in addition to the emotional level. You can build relationships with your customers that are real, open, and honest with them if you have a good customer-focus strategy. It also shows you how to set up the right tools and procedures to accomplish this. Here are six suggestions for keeping process improvement and relationship management top of mind at the same time:

1.) Encourage teamwork

To become a customer-focused business, teams must collaborate to create a consistent and improved experience. In fact, more than 70% of customers expect businesses to work together for them.

Sales teams and support teams might work together like this:

*A representative can flag selling when a buyer has interest in learning about a new product.

 *A sales rep can redirect a more technical question to an agent who specializes in that area

Furthermore, Benchmark research demonstrates that sales and support teams that collaborate have:

*More leads

*more deals

* more deals closed

However, collaboration should not slow down the productivity of your teams because it only complicates things for the customer. As a result, a connective layer that connects customer data across departments is necessary for efficient customer collaboration. Teams are able to share their insights without:

Exposing the customer to what's going on behind the scenes and disrupting their workflow.

The modern method of selling

2.) Make sure your clients feel heard.

There is a story behind every customer. However, customers do not want to hear that story over and over again whenever they interact with your brand. Additionally, customers will likely not remember your business as customer-focused if they feel ignored because they must repeat themselves.

"Making the customer feel heard is a huge part of customer focus." And the experience can quickly go wrong when they don't feel heard.

Imagine having to reintroduce yourself to a coworker each time you see them in the kitchen of the office and remind them of what you discussed the previous time you spoke to them. Although this is frequently how businesses communicate with their customers, it is neither personal nor focused on the customer.

Businesses will require the same connective tissue in order to guarantee that their clients are pleased and feel heard. This provides them with the complete customer profile.

This provides teams with the relevant context and conversation history they need to provide customers with the personalized experiences they expect
. *Their name
*Account information
*When they last reached out

3.) Take your clients where they are.

It may appear to be simpler to concentrate on a single communication channel and provide an excellent experience there. However, a significant factor in customer loyalty is the ability to communicate with them through their preferred channels.

The data are abundant: An easy customer experience is a great one. Customers shouldn't have to work hard to reach your brand, either. Companies with a focus on customers meet their customers where they are. Customers are free to contact us at any time thanks to this.

It can be eye-opening to examine your customers' demographics and the most frequently asked questions. You might be advised to offer a particular channel by industry best practices. However, you might find that a lot of your customers would rather use a mobile-first option. Because your customers are on mobile devices, you might want to consider adding WhatsApp, SMS, or another mobile messaging channel.

Once more, connecting conversations across channels will require a 360-degree view of the customer. It ensures that the customer moves with the context. This enables your company to respond to inquiries promptly and personally, regardless of when or how they contact you.

4.) Use feedback to improve

Knowing how to respond to feedback from customers is another important part of becoming a customer-focused business. Companies with a focus on customers don't treat customer complaints like a dodgeball game. Instead, they:

*Utilize customer feedback to improve the customer experience, including the following:

*Sending surveys to your customers

  * creating an online community where they can vote on new feature requests and share their product or service experiences. These are important ways to keep your customers in the loop. Like any healthy

relationship, your relationship with them should have both sides.

one of the first steps to creating a customer-focused culture is to treat customers like partners and collaborators rather than consumers of your goods."

5.) Combine data and empathy

With the growing amount of data available, businesses no longer have to guess or decide for their customers. They can instead follow the trends.

However, using data blindly is not necessary when taking a customer-focused approach. Instead, it involves combining empathy and data. This entails:

*Insights into who is using your product and what they're looking for can be gained by adding context to the data, *applying the data in a compassionate manner,

*using the data to improve customer intimacy.

To ensure that change is relevant to those it affects, your product team might, for instance, align a product update with data on customer support. Or, rather than sending the same email to each customer, a marketing team might:

*Segment content based on what emails a customer has previously opened

 *Regulate content accordingly so that each person is in the customer journey

*siloed data frequently prevents businesses from using it effectively and in a way that truly benefits the customer. That's because they don't have enough information to do so. In order to effectively manage and interpret the data, you will need to connect insights across software and systems at the outset.

Businesses become more human brands that are driven by relationships rather than profits or requirements when they begin to focus more on their customers. Try shifting your attention to the customer if your business wants to increase customer loyalty. With just a shift in mindset, you might be surprised at what you can accomplish.

Chapter 5

Learn to pay attention

Active listening is a communication technique that aims to help two or more people understand each other. It is frequently used in sales, coaching, and teaching professions. Both parties benefit from the communication by having their needs, wants, and desires heard through active listening.

The goal of active listening is to find common ground between two or more parties, which is why it is important. Since it's nearly impossible to sell anything in sales if you can't agree on the problem and solution by the end of the conversation, active listening is essential.

However, active listening is not as straightforward as turning on our ears and mimicking a mockingbird by repeating everything we hear to the other person. There is a method for effectively engaging in active listening.

1. Be aware of the requirements of the prospective client.

2. Confirm that you are aware of the requirements of the prospect.

3. Clarify your understanding of their requirements

As we tried to persuade marketers to adopt a new marketing strategy, I found it useful to use this three-step framework to dig deeper into a prospect's requirements by asking pertinent follow-up questions.

1. Recognize the needs of the prospect.

Let's be real for a minute: We sometimes listen for a word or a topic that perfectly leads us to our next thought during a conversation.

Even though this isn't rude, offensive, or otherwise problematic, it does make it harder for us to have conversations that make us think.

Prospects can sense this when salespeople do this, and they conclude that the representative simply wants to sell them something regardless of whether they need it or not. It's a downward spiral that almost never ends.

However, the most effective salespeople listen differently. They really listen to what a prospect is saying and feeling through their language, tone of voice, facial expressions, and body language, ignoring the script and possibly even their own agenda.

A salesperson can truly begin to comprehend the plight of their prospect and put themselves in the buyer's shoes by observing the prospect's words as well as their auditory, visual, and physical clues.

Additionally, active listening, a form of listening, has the potential to have a significant impact by encouraging prospects to open up more and fostering trust and commitment.

So, when you're talking to a prospect over the phone or in a meeting, don't pay attention to anything else, forget about the script, and don't worry about what you'll say next.

2. Confirm that you are aware of the requirements of the prospect.

Frequently, this crucial step is overlooked. Simply ask, "Did I communicate that effectively?" after paraphrasing your prospect's words. or, "Do you feel I fully understand what you said to me?" If the prospect responds with a "no," you can now ask,

"Could you clarify for me what I might have missed or understood incorrectly?"

Take note of how those questions open the door for them to provide you with honest feedback. Conversely, I do not advocate asking, "Does that make sense?" or "Could you describe that more clearly?" or any question that assigns the prospect's communication struggle to them.

You will be able to induce a confirmation bias in your prospect's mind once you have mastered this step. Confirmation bias begins to develop and trust begins to grow when you repeat what this person has said and confirm that you are on the same page.

3. Make sure you know what they need.

The next thing you should do is follow up with questions after you have established that you comprehend the prospect.

Avoid asking closed-ended questions because doing so could give the impression to the prospect that you are only interested in making a sale. Instead, I suggest asking your prospect an open-ended question that prompts them to elaborate on their objectives, challenges, and current plans.

The person is free to say what they thinks in their own words when open-ended questions are asked. Prospects may solve their own problems or at least begin to believe that there is a solution if they ask the right questions. They might even come to the conclusion that your approach is the best one. In addition, you have a better chance of discovering the compelling reasons your prospect will (or will not) buy from you if you encourage them to continue critically considering their situation.

On your next call, this framework for active listening will give you the basic tools you need to start actively listening, but the strategies below will help you get to the end and close the deal.

Strategies for Enhancing Your Active Listening

1. Set the mood.

Before the conversation begins, clearly state what you and the other person will discuss. This sets the tone. This should set reasonable expectations for both of you so that neither party feels like their time was wasted. Keep in mind that mutual understanding is the goal of active listening, and the best way to do this is to set the tone right away.

2. Concentrate on body language

Body language conveys information that the voice cannot. This applies to both parties: how you use body language can not only inform you of how they are feeling but also have an impact on the conversation. Always pay close attention to their movements, expressions, and eyes. But also pay attention to how enthusiastic you are being. Keeping a friendly, upbeat, and curious demeanor can go a long way toward finding common ground.

3. Find connections between ideas

Active listening focuses on identifying the needs of the other party and coming up with a path forward together, rather than listening to respond. Making connections between ideas not only demonstrates to the other person that you are listening to them but also positions you as an expert in your field with a lot of experience solving problems similar to theirs.

4. Instead of focusing on differences, look for opportunities.

Try to refocus the conversation on opportunities, even if you are convinced that the prospect is making a poor decision. Consider, for instance, asking them about the sources they consulted to verify their decisions and the factors that influenced them. Then, give people a chance to see your product or service through that same lens.

These examples demonstrate that Active Listening is a skill that can be utilized at almost any stage of the sales process, from the initial interaction to the final transaction.

Chapter 6:

Sales funnel

The sales funnel is the process that prospective customers go through before making a purchase. A sales funnel typically consists of the top, middle, and bottom steps; however, these steps may differ depending on a company's sales model.

Any business owner is aware of the agony of missing out on a sale. The prospect leaves the sales funnel without making a purchase after weeks of sales pitches, demonstrations, and charm.

It occurs. However, with the appropriate support for sales funnel management, it occurs less frequently. Patchwork spreadsheets, sticky notes, missed appointments, and forgotten follow-ups leave holes in many small business sales funnels, making them look more like sieves.

There is a superior method. Software for sales and marketing automation can fill in the gaps in the sales funnel and convert near-misses into sales.

What is the purpose of the sales funnel?

Understanding what potential customers are thinking and doing throughout the buying process is made easier by a sales funnel. You can use these insights to invest in the right marketing activities and channels, create the most relevant messages at each stage and convert more potential customers into paying clients.

What are the stages of the sales funnel?

Prospects move through various stages of your sales funnel, beginning when they hear about your product or service and ending when they either buy it or don't. While each prospect's journey through your funnel may differ, they will ultimately evaluate it based on their level of interest. They will consider the issue they are attempting to resolve and conduct research on rival products to ensure that your solution is superior.

There are generally four main stages:

Stage 1: Awareness

Due to the point at which people first become aware of your product or service, the first stage of the sales funnel is referred to as the "awareness" level. They might find out about you through your advertising, social media, or even recommendations.

Naturally, your own sales and marketing skills determine how and why these people move down the sales funnel. Because they have moved beyond awareness to interest, the leads in the middle and lower stages of the sales funnel are the ones you want to pay the most attention to.

A prospect learning about your company for the first time is an example of the awareness stage. They might have heard a coworker talk about your product or service, read your blog, found your website through a Google search, or clicked on one of your ads.

Stage 2: Interest

After learning about your brand, prospects will evaluate it based on their level of interest. They will consider the issue they are attempting to resolve and conduct research on rival products to ensure that your solution is superior.

Stage 3: Decision

Prospects will investigate your pricing and packaging options more thoroughly once they have information about your business. At this stage, sales pages, webinars, and phone calls can be helpful in convincing potential customers to buy.

Stage 4: Action

This stage is the culmination of all of your work: whether or not the prospect buys something. The deal isn't lost forever if they didn't. To ensure that you remain in people's minds, you can create nurture campaigns.

How to Make a Sales Funnel for Your Company

Before you can have a sales funnel, you need prospects who can go through it. Using lead scoring, you can track behavior and engagement with those prospects to determine where they are in the sales funnel.

To help you make a sales funnel, follow these five steps:

1. Create a landing page

A landing page is probably the first place prospects will learn about your business. A landing page will open up when they download an ebook, sign up for a webinar, or click on an advertisement. Because this may be the one and only chance you have to impress potential customers, that page ought to make it abundantly clear who your business is and the distinct advantages it offers. Lastly, and most importantly, ensure that the landing page contains a form for prospects to fill out. You want to get their email address so you can keep in touch with them.

2. Offer something valuable

This is the part where you have to give your prospects something in return for their email address. An effective way to provide something of value on your landing page is through a lead magnet, such as an ebook or whitepaper.

3. Start nurturing.

At this point, your prospects will be in the Interest stage, which is the next stage up from awareness. Additionally, since you have all of their email addresses from the landing page, you can develop an email nurture series to distribute instructional content regarding your product or service.

4. Upsell:

When prospects reach the Decision stage, you should offer anything that might nudge them to make a purchase. A product demonstration, extended free trial, or special discount are all examples of this.

5. Keep going

During the Action phase, you'll either discover why prospects aren't interested in making a purchase or acquiring new customers. In either case, maintain communication. Focus on product education, engagement, and retention for new customers. Create a new nurture series to check in with prospects who did not make a purchase every few months.

Identifying the gaps in your sales funnel stages

Now that you know how to build a sales funnel, we can begin to understand why sales funnel management is important. If they are not carefully nurtured, even very good prospects can slip out of the sales funnel along the way. Having a clear understanding of the steps in your sales process and contributing to their completion is the best way to avoid that loss.

Everything you do to get people into the first stage of your sales funnel is called prospecting and marketing. Keep in mind that whenever possible, stages are divided into two or more steps. A demo may be referred to as a single

stage, but in reality, it entails numerous components, including doing the demonstration, sending reminders, contacting the customer, and then following up. Support for managing your sales funnel stages will remain the same, regardless of how they differ from one another.

Once you know the stages of your sales funnel, it's time to figure out where potential customers are leaving. If you are the CEO, CMO, and head janitor, sit down with your team and ask yourself:

*Where are my sales process's bottlenecks?

*Where do I typically lose track of prospective clients?

*What are the positive trigger points, or the particular actions that typically lead to a sale?

Pay close attention to the cracks where your chosen steps might not be effective. Prepare to fix your funnel then.

There are three primary causes of leaks in the sales funnel process. The good news is that the management of sales funnels can assist with each.

Putting the "no's" away too quickly

In sales, a "no" can frequently mean "not until later." For instance, the following is a common criticism of customer relationship management (CRM) software: I lack the time to put together my content to make the platform useful. In actuality, this prospect is saying, "I'm interested, I see the value, but I can't take advantage of it right now."

It would be nice to give up on this lead and move on to the next one.

A better option exists: Create an automated email follow-up campaign that addresses this objection directly. You can send that prospect information that appears to be tailored just for them whenever you encounter this issue. Their content anxiety may be reduced and they may be encouraged toward a sale by a campaign that lasts for a long time. Despite the initial effort, this campaign will continue to benefit you.

Task item: Consider which of your prospects' most common objections can be resolved through helpful education and automated follow-up. Where in your sales funnel do you dismiss potential customers too quickly?

Failures in follow-up

Are you doing your best ? Probably not, given that: *80% of sales require five follow-ups; *44% of sales representatives give up after one follow-up; *46% of leads require 3-5 touchpoints before becoming qualified prospects. The difficulty is simple to comprehend:

Do I call brand-new leads or call an existing lead for the sixth time? The numbers demonstrate that persistence is not a waste of time.

However, there is a better option: A funnel for marketing automation may be of assistance to small businesses. At each stage of the sales funnel, all of your prospects receive friendly, consistent emails and contacts, allowing you to concentrate on the day's most active leads.

Task item: Examine your 20 most recent leads and keep track of the average number of times you contacted a prospect. A marketing automation funnel can be helpful if you notice that follow-up fails.

Too slow

Did you know that if you follow up with new leads within the first five minutes after they express interest, their chances of converting are nine times higher? Your lead's likelihood of becoming a sale is 21 times lower if you wait more than 30 minutes.

You might be wondering, "How in the world am I supposed to contact a lead within the first five minutes?" That doesn't seem possible.

A better option exists: With automation for sales funnel management, it's not impossible. If you set up your system with the response you want, it will be ready to send it to any interested prospect right away, even if they call you at 3 in the morning on a Saturday. Your sales automation platform can send added personalized emails that are just right for each moment as captured leads move down the funnel.

Task item: Determine your usual response time to a new prospect right now. Then, create your first mass, customized email to send to potential customers.

Send the right message to the right people at the right time in the sales funnel

How do automated emails move through the sales funnel?

Let's say your sales pitch is frequently met with two distinct objections: "We're not sure we need it," and "We don't have time to implement." You can compose a series of emails to respond to each one and schedule their delivery over the coming weeks or months.

You might want to send different materials at different times depending on the objection: testimonials from other customers, instructional videos that demonstrate how simple it is to set up your system, or just friendly email updates.

Now, every stage of your marketing automation funnel is helping you: Within five minutes of their initial contact, it responded, which facilitated your opportunity to present your pitch. After the pitch, you are now prepared to maintain contact and respond politely and specifically to objections. Automation can also help you keep in touch with them until the deal is closed if they like the pitch.)

A customer relationship management system is best in this situation. Every piece of information in your database can be pulled into a good CRM, allowing you to make each email completely unique.

Management of a sales funnel involves more than just being organized. It's about giving each potential client the individual attention they deserve. It all boils down to doing so consistently at the appropriate times. so that you can devote more of your time to the activity that provides the greatest reward: finishing deals.

Conclusion

If you are the owner of a business and do not prioritize increasing sales, your company may not be as profitable as you had hoped. A business becomes a hobby or a charitable organization if no products or services are sold. Within the organization, sales are not just the responsibility of the sales force. At every department level, everyone must understand how sales can and do occur.

It's great to have a great storefront, great products, and a fun mascot, but without sales, these things are just costs that make an organization lose money. The majority of business leaders have distinct strategies for each marketing channel because sales come from a variety of sources. An online sales funnel, for instance, could sell products without a salesperson. However, the efficiency with which the order is fulfilled contributes to closing the deal. The storefront, inventory, and mascot are paid for by sales, so this is important.

A company's size, margin, and profitability increase when its owner is able to effectively increase sales without significantly increasing costs per sale. When a company is scaled up, the owners may be able to obtain discounts for advertising, delivery, and larger quantities of inventory through economies of scale. This indicates that the company could double its sales but not its expenses, increasing profitability.
Everyone, including the mascot, is better able to carry out their role in the sales process when they are aware of it. People are better able to carry out job responsibilities when they are aware of what is expected of them. Not only is this a recipe for

success at work, but it also increases job satisfaction. A positive corporate culture is created when a lot of employees are content. This scenario is inextricably linked to sales.

For instance, the representative for customer service typically deals with dissatisfied clients. It might be a job with little reward and little job satisfaction. However, on the off chance that the job is characterized as client maintenance trained professional and the delegate is given the instruments to take care of issues, he could not just satisfy the client toward the finish of the call yet additionally he could possibly sell another item or to update the current item. Even though the customer service representative is not a salesperson, she or he demonstrates how these representatives can help retain customers and increase product sales.

Good customer service makes clients who might otherwise be dissatisfied happy. However, client retention is not just about keeping sales. The customer experience must be considered in the sales process by business owners. The customer experience is typically positive if the sales process is positive. Advertising of product and service positioning are the first steps in the sales process.

The sales representative is then in charge of the procedure; It matters what he says and how he says it. He cannot be overly assertive or make exaggerated claims if the process is to remain positive.

www.ingramcontent.com/pod-product-compliance
Lightning Source LLC
Chambersburg PA
CBHW070749220526
45467CB00018B/1657